A Walk With Granny

Nigel Gray

Illustrations by
Jason Walker

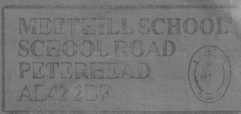

MEFFHILL SCHOOL
SCHOOL ROAD
PETERHEAD
AB42 2BF

CAMBRIDGE
UNIVERSITY PRESS

Cambridge Reading

General Editors
Richard Brown and Kate Ruttle

Consultant Editor
Jean Glasberg

PUBLISHED BY THE PRESS SYNDICATE OF THE UNIVERSITY OF CAMBRIDGE
The Pitt Building, Trumpington Street, Cambridge CB2 1RP, United Kingdom

CAMBRIDGE UNIVERSITY PRESS
The Edinburgh Building, Cambridge CB2 2RU, United Kingdom
40 West 20th Street, New York, NY 10011-4211, USA
10 Stamford Road, Oakleigh, Melbourne 3166, Australia

Text © Nigel Gray 1998
Cover and text illustrations © Jason Walker 1998

This book is in copyright. Subject to statutory exception and to the provisions of relevant collective licensing agreements,
no reproduction of any part may take place without the written permission of Cambridge University Press.

First published 1998

Printed in the United Kingdom at the University Press, Cambridge

Typeset in Perpetua

A catalogue record for this book is available from the British Library

ISBN 0 521 46928 7 paperback

It was a sunny day. After lunch, Joe's mum went out in the car. Mike did the washing-up. Mike had just moved in to live with Joe's mum. He was trying to be nice to Joe, trying to be like a dad to him. Joe's real dad had gone away when Joe was small. Joe couldn't remember him.

"Do you want to go for a walk?" asked Mike.

"If you like," said Joe. "Where to?"

"Just down the track," said Mike. "We have to take Flea."

Flea was Joe's granny's dog. Joe's Granny Beth had died. Now, Joe and his mum and Mike had to look after Flea.

Flea was small. She was old, and rather fat. Granny Beth had been a bit like that too.

"Do you want your shoes on?" asked Mike.

"No," said Joe.

"Are you sure?" asked Mike. "The road will be hot."

"I'm sure," said Joe.

"The track is stony," said Mike.

"I know," said Joe. "I often go there. My feet are like leather."

They walked along the side of the road. There was no path. Flea followed them. They turned down the track. It was cooler there. There were some trees and bushes, which gave shade.

In some places, there were still puddles from the recent rain, and some patches of wet mud. Joe liked the feel of the wet mud under his feet. He liked to squidge it between his toes.

"Yuk," said Mike.

Where the trees ended, the track was hot and dry. Flea walked more and more slowly. She was uncomfortable inside her thick fur coat. She panted, and her tongue hung out.

"Come on, Flea," Mike said. "Get a move on."

"She's old," said Joe.

"Her legs are too short," said Mike. "What's the use of a dog with such little legs? A dog should be able to go for long walks."

"I think Granny Beth had little legs," said Joe. "She didn't like going for long walks."

Flea sat down on the track.

"Come on, Flea," said Mike.

Flea didn't budge.

"I'll get her," Joe said. "She knows me."

Joe went back and stroked Flea. "Come on, Flea," he said. "Come with me."

Flea rolled onto her back. All four legs were in the air.

"Leave her," said Mike. "She'll follow soon."

"Come on, Flea," said Joe.

Joe made Flea roll back onto her tummy.

She jumped up and snapped at him.

"What a snappy dog," said Mike.

"Granny Beth was snappy sometimes," said Joe.

Mike and Joe walked on, side by side.
Flea followed, slowly, reluctantly. The sun was hot.
Joe took off his shirt.

"Mind, you'll burn," said Mike.

"Mum's always telling me that," said Joe.

"She's right," said Mike. "I go red, then my skin
peels off."

"Yuk," said Joe.

There was a snail on the track.

Joe stopped to look at it. Mike walked on.

The snail had two little horns on its head.

Joe put out a finger to touch the horns.

The snail withdrew its horns into its head.

It withdrew itself into its shell.

Joe tried to pick it up.

The snail clung to the ground.

Joe pulled harder.

He lifted the snail and put

it in the grass at the

side of the track.

"You'll be safe there," Joe said to the snail.

"You won't get squashed there."

Mike strolled along the track. Joe followed a
little way behind. Some way behind Joe, came Flea.

Joe came to an electric fence. Attached to the fence
was a box with an electric motor inside. It sounded
like a huge clock ticking. A cow came to the fence. It
looked at Joe with sad eyes. There were lots of flies
around its eyes. Its eyes looked red and sore. It looked
as though it had been crying.

"Poor cow," said Joe. "I'm sorry your eyes are sore."

Mike was a long way ahead. Joe felt
like running. He ran along the track as fast
as he could.

He was in a race. The winning post was
a dead tree. He was number eight.
Eight was his favourite number.
He nearly won, but number
twelve just beat him.
Number twelve won
by three paces.
Joe was second.

Joe was hot from running. He pushed his hair back
from his face. His hair was wet. He heard a tractor.
He looked back. Flea was far behind. She was sitting
in the middle of the track. A red tractor was coming
along behind her.

Joe took a deep breath, and straight away became Super Joe. He had to reach Flea before she was killed by the tractor. He ran back. He had super powers. He was flying through the air faster than the speed of sound.

The tractor driver saw Joe running towards him. He saw Flea in the middle of the track. He slowed down.

Joe ran up to Flea and scooped her up. Flea growled at him.
"It's all right, Flea," Joe said. "Super Joe will save your life."
Joe stood in the long grass at the side of the track. The tractor
came past.

The driver looked grumpy. Joe smiled and waved. Then the
driver smiled too, and waved back. The tractor passed on down
the track, raising a little cloud of dust.

Joe put Flea down at the side of the track. Flea sat down. Joe saw that Mike was coming back. He squatted beside Flea and scratched behind her ears.

"Hi," said Mike.

"Hi," said Joe.

"There's a nice old house down there," said Mike.

"I know," said Joe. "I might buy it one day and live there."

"Shall we go back home?" asked Mike.

"If you like," said Joe. "Flea doesn't want to go any further."

"What's that on your leg?" asked Mike, pointing.

Joe tried to see what was on the back of his leg.

"It's a grasshopper," said Mike. Mike gently lifted the grasshopper off Joe's leg. "Look," he said.

He put the grasshopper onto Joe's hand. It was bright green. It had big eyes and long legs. It sat very still. Joe looked at it for a long time.

"It's great," Joe said.

"It can give you a nip," said Mike.

"Would it hurt?" Joe asked.

"A bit," Mike said.

Joe put the grasshopper in the long grass at the side of the track. The grasshopper hopped.

"Where did it go?" asked Joe.

"I didn't see," said Mike.

Joe searched for it, but it was nowhere to be seen.

They walked back along the track. Flea knew she was going home. She ran beside them.

"She's happy now," Mike said.

"I don't think she's happy," Joe said.

"Why not?" asked Mike.

"She misses Granny Beth," Joe said.

"Ah, yes," said Mike. "Of course. Do you miss her too?"

"Yes," said Joe. "A bit. She was my only granny."

"Listen!" said Mike. They stopped walking. Flea sat down. She was panting. Her tongue was hanging out.

"What is it?" asked Joe.

"A wood duck," Mike told him.

"It sounds like a cat," Joe said.

Mike laughed. "Yes," he said. "It does. And it nests in a tree. One night, when I was a boy, I took my flashlight and climbed into a tree where some wood ducks were roosting. I could hear this miaowing — and I thought a cat was stuck up there."

"We had a cat once," Joe said. "But it died."

"What did it die of?" asked Mike.

"I think it was just old," Joe said. "Like Granny Beth."

Joe picked a grass from the side of the track. "This is the tree in summer," he said, holding the grass up to Mike. He slid his fingers up the stem of the grass, pulling off the fluffy seed heads. "This is the tree in winter," he said. He showed Mike the bare grass stem. "This is a bunch of flowers," he said, showing the seeds still bunched on his fingers.

"This is the April showers," he said. He threw the grass seeds up into Mike's face. Joe laughed. Mike laughed too. "That's a good little rhyme," he said. "Where did you learn that?"

"Granny Beth taught it to me when I was small,"
Joe told him.

They walked on. They passed the electric fence, which was still ticking. Two cows stopped grazing to watch them pass.

Joe picked up another sort of grass. The seed head was long and fat and green. "It's like a caterpillar," he said. "A fat, green caterpillar."

"You can keep it for a pet," Mike said.

"I had a caterpillar once," said Joe. "I kept it in a jar and gave it fresh leaves every day. One morning, it had made itself a cocoon. It was changing into a butterfly. I wanted to see the butterfly coming out of the cocoon. But I left the lid off the jar so it would have some air, and one day I looked in, and the butterfly had gone. I never saw it."

"What a shame," said Mike. "Never mind. We can find another caterpillar next spring."

"Will you still be here next spring?" asked Joe.

"Sure," said Mike. "I'm not going anywhere."

They came back into the shade of the trees.
"That's better," Mike said. "It's not so hot here."

"I like it hot," Joe said.

Flea ran on ahead. She began drinking from
a muddy puddle.

"Yuk," said Mike.

They reached the road and turned towards home.
"When you were a child, did you have a granny?"
Joe asked.

"No," Mike said. "No. I didn't."

"That's a shame," Joe said.

"Yes," Mike said.

"Look!" said Joe. "The car's there. Mum must be back."

Mum met them at the door.

"Hello," she said. "Where have you been?"

"We took Flea for a walk," Joe said.

"Just you and Mike?" she asked.

Joe hesitated. Then, "Yes," he said. "Just me and Mike."

Flea flopped down onto the rug.
Joe knelt beside her. She began licking
his hand.

Joe and Mike looked at each other,
and smiled.